THE FLIGHT OF THE LONE EAGLE

In the middle 1920s "Atlantic fever," a rage to fly across the ocean, sprang up in both the United States and Europe. The watery graveyard took the lives of many intrepid men and women, but there were always other valiants eager to try their luck. Most of the aircraft used for the transatlantic flight were big two- and three-motor ships with crews of from two to five. One, the *Spirit of St. Louis*, was a small, single-engine monoplane whose pilot, Charles A. Lindbergh, flew her alone. At dawn on May 20, 1927, he took off from Roosevelt Field on Long Island, New York, for Paris, France, 3,600 miles away. The outcome of the Lindbergh flight had far-reaching consequences in the history of the world.

PRINCIPALS

CHARLES A. LINDBERGH, the "Lone Eagle," a young airmail pilot and Air National Guard captain, who one moonlight autumn night began to dream of flying alone from New York to Paris.

MRS. EVANGELINE LODGE LAND LINDBERGH, the pilot's mother, who barnstormed with him and who, badly worried by the sensational stories about the upcoming flight that were appearing in the press, came to be with her son before he took off.

RAYMOND ORTEIG, a Paris-born New York hotel owner, who put up a $25,000 prize for a nonstop flight between New York and Paris.

HARRY BRUNO, a flier and public relations man, who drove his roadster with a fire extinguisher aboard behind Lindbergh's plane when she roared down the runway on the transatlantic flight.

HARRY KNIGHT, a young St. Louis broker, to whom Lindbergh turned in desperation when trying to find backers for his flight.

COMMANDER RICHARD E. BYRD of the United States Navy, a competitor of Lindbergh's, who had leased Roosevelt Field but permitted the young pilot to use it.

THE *Spirit of St. Louis*, probably the most famous aircraft ever made, a high-wing, single-engine monoplane, designed for and built around her pilot, which took on near-human qualities.

A FOCUS BOOK

The Flight of the Lone Eagle

*Charles Lindbergh
Flies Nonstop from
New York to Paris*

By John T. Foster

FRANKLIN WATTS, INC.
NEW YORK / 1974

The authors and publisher of the Focus Books wish to acknowledge the helpful editorial suggestions of Professor Richard B. Morris.

The quotations in this book not otherwise identified are from *The Spirit of St. Louis* by Charles A. Lindbergh and are reprinted with the permission of Charles Scribner's Sons.

Photo research by Selma Hamdan
Cover by Ginger Giles

Library of Congress Cataloging in Publication Data

Foster, John T
    The flight of the Lone Eagle.

    (A Focus book)
    SUMMARY: An account of the first solo nonstop transatlantic flight, made by Charles Lindbergh in 1927 in *The Spirit of St. Louis,* an event which marked the beginning of the Air Age.
    Bibliography: p.
    1. Lindbergh, Charles Augustus, 1902–   –Juvenile literature. 2. Transatlantic flights–Juvenile literature. [1. Lindbergh, Charles Augustus, 1902–
2. Transatlantic flights] I. Title.
TL540.L5F65   629.13'092'4 [B] [92]   74–898
ISBN 0-531-02723-6

Picture credits:

Library of Congress pp. ii, viii, 21, 22, 25, 28, 31, 49, 54-55; RCA p. 6B; National Baseball Library p. 7A; U.S. Information Agency pp. 6A, 7B, 16, 46; U.S. Air Force pp. 13, 14; State Historical Society of Wisconsin pp. 19, 50; U.S. Navy, National Archives p. 34.

Contents

For R. J. Foster

*The Flight
of the
Lone Eagle*

Charles Lindbergh in the window of his plane in May, 1927.

Alone

Charles A. Lindbergh gazed out at the rain glumly. He had spent a sleepless night, and now a wet dawn was approaching. Although only twenty-five years old, "Slim" Lindbergh, as he was known to his friends, had logged nearly 2,000 hours in the air—barnstorming, wing-walking, parachute-jumping, flying the mail—and was one of the best aviators in the world, no matter what anybody said. But now this tall, lean boyish-looking man was planning to take off in a small, single-engine monoplane on a flight from New York to Paris, and he was going alone.

It was May 20, 1927. Lindbergh was standing with a group of mechanics, policemen, reporters, and friends in a hangar at Curtiss Field, Long Island, New York. Nearby was the flier's plane, the *Spirit of St. Louis*. In this fragile ship of steel, wood, and fabric, Lindbergh proposed to make the 3,600-mile flight to Le Bourget Field outside Paris.

The young mail pilot from Detroit, Michigan, and St. Louis, Missouri, was not the first to attempt a flight between New York and Paris (although no one had ever before tried it alone). During the middle 1920s, in pursuit of a $25,000 prize offered by a Paris-born New York City hotel owner named Raymond Orteig, many brave men on both sides of the Atlantic had tried to make the epochal flight. None had been successful. A number had died— some horribly.

Lindbergh had faced death on many occasions—like the time he had been forced to bail out of an aircraft that was in an ir- reversible tailspin. Floating down in his parachute, he had looked up to see the plane close by and headed in his direction. It had passed within a few feet of him before crashing.

He was hardly a "Flyin' Fool," as one New York newspaper had dubbed him. He was well aware of the many problems and complications of a transatlantic flight, and the consequences of failure—a fiery death if he crashed at takeoff or landing, a watery death if he went down somewhere in between. He would have to fight fatigue, sleep, fog, and perhaps storms all the way. If he lost to any of these opponents . . .

But Lindbergh had confidence in his own ability, developed out of a childhood interest in mechanics and an involvement with aviation as an adult that had led him to stunt flying and parachute jumping as well as his year of experience in carrying the mail by air under all possible flying conditions.

Other fliers had flown across the Atlantic. In May, 1919, four mammoth flying boats from the U.S. Navy, each carrying a five-man crew, set out from Newfoundland for the Azores. At sixty-mile intervals across the ocean the Navy had stationed destroyers, each sending out radio signals and shooting up star shells to guide the airmen. And yet, despite all the preparations and precautions, only one flying boat actually made the 1,380-mile flight (although all the crews of the downed planes were rescued).

The following June, two British fliers, Captain John Alcock and Lieutenant Arthur Brown, took off from St. John's, Newfoundland, in a twin-engine biplane and flew 1,936 miles to Clifden, Ireland, crash-landing in a bog.

But Lindbergh would be attempting a flight nearly twice as long as the Britishers', and he had no fleet of destroyers out there in the Atlantic, waiting to guide him across the ocean with star shells and radio signals.

For that matter, he had no radio. When the *Spirit of St. Louis* was being designed and built for him, Lindbergh decided that he would rather have an extra 90 pounds of fuel than a radio. He had long before that decided he would rather have an extra 170 pounds or so of fuel than a copilot or navigator.

For fuel, he had sacrificed every bit of weight he could control. He had gone to the extent of cutting out of his maps the areas over which he didn't expect to fly and ripping off the extra pages in his logbook.

Because he couldn't fly the highly sensitive *Spirit of St. Louis* and get an accurate sighting with a sextant at the same time, Lindbergh had decided to go without that instrument. He would navigate by dead reckoning—estimating the position of his plane not by astronomical observation but by applying to a previously determined position the course and distance traveled since that point.

To save weight for fuel, Lindbergh was not even carrying a parachute. If he had to ditch his plane at sea, he had a small rubber life raft—weight: ten pounds.

Fully loaded with 450 gallons of gasoline, the *Spirit of St. Louis* weighed 5,250 pounds. That was 115 pounds more than she had been designed to lift, but Lindbergh had confidence in her.

It was a little after 3:00 A.M. The rain, a light drizzle from low clouds, kept coming down. Visibility was poor, the field soft and muddy. Conditions could be better for such a flight.

On the other hand, the weatherman had reported that a low pressure area over Nova Scotia and Newfoundland was receding, along with its fog, and a high pressure area was over most of the North Atlantic. Except for local storms on the French coast, the route would probably be clear—*probably*. Another point: the moon had just passed full and each night would be more on the wane. Lindbergh needed that light.

"Bring her out," he told the mechanics.

They wheeled the *Spirit of St. Louis* out of the hangar and tied her tail to a truck, wrapping a tarpaulin around the nose to protect the engine from the rain. The truck started the short trip to Roosevelt Field, adjoining Curtiss to the east, hauling the plane backwards like a dead bull being dragged from an arena.

Gazing at his ship, Lindbergh thought she looked utterly incapable of flying. He and the others began to slog through the mud behind her. To the pilot, it seemed more like a funeral procession than the beginning of a flight to Paris.

The Whoopee Years

In 1903 there occurred two events that had a profound effect upon the United States and the world during the second decade of the twentieth century and thereafter. On June 14 of that year, Henry Ford founded the Ford Motor Company in Detroit, Michigan, operating in a converted icehouse. Then on December 17, at Kitty Hawk, North Carolina, a bicycle repairman named Orville Wright flew a power-driven airplane a few feet off the ground for twelve seconds while his brother Wilbur trotted alongside.

Thanks largely to Ford, the automobile would no longer be the toy of the rich. Families began to live in the new suburbs, the man of the house either driving to work or to the depot where he took the train to his job.

During the First World War aviation was stimulated, and planes were used, at first for reconnaissance and later in bombing and aerial combat. Many advances took place in airplane design and manufacturing.

During the 1920s America's culture was undergoing a revolution. Led by their women, the American people were rebelling against puritanism and fuddy-duddies. Women were bobbing their hair. Skirts became shorter.

Tired and disillusioned after World War I, people wanted to have some fun. They had it with hip flasks and speakeasies (from "speak easily," meaning "carefully," a place for the illegal sale of alcoholic drinks). Prohibition had been in effect since the war, but people were tired of that, too.

A popular expression then was "It's later than you think," and America played like mad. The automobile gave her sons and daughters greater opportunity for play. People were frenziedly dancing the Charleston and the Black Bottom, and singing such nonsense songs as "Yes, We Have No Bananas" and "Barney Google" ("with his goo-goo-googly eyes").

Calvin—"Silent Cal"—Coolidge was president. Although he was a champion of thrift and propriety when his fellow Americans were living fast and loose, Coolidge was highly popular. America savored his infrequent statements, such as "Let men in public office substitute the light that comes from the midnight oil for the limelight."

His fellow Americans much preferred the limelight, idolizing sports figures, movie stars, any type of hero or heroine—pseudo or otherwise; even gangsters like Al "Scarface" Capone were celebrities. In 1926 Jack Dempsey, the most popular American prizefighter since John L. Sullivan, lost the heavyweight crown to a Shakespeare-quoting ex-Marine named Gene Tunney. That same year the American long-distance swimmer Gertrude Ederle became the first woman to swim the English Channel. She achieved her feat in fourteen hours and thirty-one minutes, beating the men's record by nearly two and a half hours. In baseball it was George Herman "Babe" Ruth, a bull-shouldered, skinny-shanked right fielder who hit a record sixty home runs in 1927.

The motion picture industry had recently come in, manufacturing new heroes and heroines. Everything the stars did and said on and off the silver screen was news. Clara Bow, the red-headed "It" girl, zipped around Hollywood in her red convertible accompanied by her seven red chow dogs—to the delight of the nation. When Rudolph Valentino, the great lover of the silent screen, died suddenly in 1926, scores of women were injured in the hysterical mob that attended his funeral.

It should not be surprising in such a time of sky-high enthusiasms that "Atlantic fever," an obsession to fly the Atlantic Ocean, flared up among pilots in both the United States and Europe. Ray-

Over, the twenties:
Rudolph Valentino and a companion;
Listening to the radio at the country club;
Babe Ruth; Clara Bow. ·

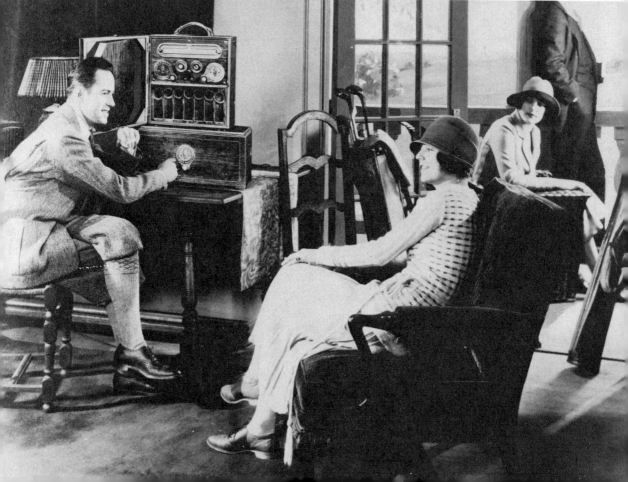

mond Orteig had first offered his prize in 1919, but it had gone unclaimed because—until the middle 1920s—there was no airplane engine that could be counted upon to run continuously for such a distance.

Then in 1926 Lieutenant Commander Richard E. Byrd of the U.S. Navy and his copilot, Floyd Bennett, became the first men to fly over the North Pole. Byrd's aircraft, a German Fokker, had three Wright Whirlwind motors, machines that proved they would be reliable for a 3,600-mile journey, and then some.

One moonlight night in September of that year, while flying the mail from Peoria, Illinois, to Chicago, the young pilot—Charles A. Lindbergh, captain in the Air National Guard—began to dream of flying to Paris.

The Spirit of St. Louis

"Why shouldn't I fly from New York to Paris?" Lindbergh asked himself, according to his book *The Spirit of St. Louis*. ". . . I have more than four years of aviation behind me, and close to two thousand hours in the air." He had barnstormed over half of the forty-eight states and flown the mail through the stormiest weather.

With the Wright Whirlwind, he had the motor. The Whirlwind was a nine-cylinder, air-cooled engine developing 220 horsepower at 1,800 revolutions per minute. It weighed 500 pounds, giving a favorable ratio of just over 2½ pounds per horsepower. Air-cooled meant no radiator filled with water, a big saving in weight; also, there was no danger of the radiator freezing or the engine overheating because of a clogged cooling system.

And with the Wright-Bellanca monoplane, or one of similar construction, he had the aircraft. Biplanes, such as those flown in World War I and the one he was using to carry the mail, wasted too much power overcoming drag.

Lindbergh also began to consider using a single-engine plane. Such an aircraft would be more liable to make forced landings, but it would have much less head resistance than a tri-motor and as a result greater cruising range. Also, a tri-motor plane had three times the chance of engine failure.

That same month the dashing French war ace, René Fonck, was making final preparations for his flight from Roosevelt Field to Le Bourget. His aircraft was a big biplane carrying three motors and a crew of four, with leather upholstery and even a bed. It had been especially designed for the flight by the famous aeronautical engineer, Igor Sikorsky.

On September 21 Fonck started down the runway for the transatlantic flight. His wheels never left the ground. At the end of the runway the lumbering biplane crashed and burst into flame.

Fonck and his copilot escaped, but the mechanic and the radio operator both burned to death.

That crash just about convinced Lindbergh that his best bet was a single-engine aircraft. Whether it had one or three motors, however, he would strip the ship of all equipment that wasn't absolutely essential, and he would fly her alone.

Where would he get the money for the plane? He could put up $2000 of his own, but he would probably need about $15,000. As he flew the mail through the winter of 1926–27, Lindbergh doggedly kept trying to get financial backing, with repeated failures. Finally, he persuaded a group of St. Louis businessmen to put up the rest of the money. The group was headed by Harry Knight, a young broker who was president of the St. Louis Flying Club.

Elated, Lindbergh wired the Travel Air Company in Kansas, ordering a monoplane.

Back came a wire refusing to accept his order.

Three other aircraft manufacturers turned him down. Obviously they all felt that his chances of success were zero and did not want their product associated with the failure. Lindbergh was beginning to get desperate. He had read of a high-wing monoplane built by a small company named Ryan Airlines in San Diego, California. On February 4, 1927, he wired Ryan asking if they could build a plane that could fly nonstop from New York to Paris; if so, how much would it cost and when could they complete it?

Next day he received a reply:

CAN BUILD PLANE SIMILAR M ONE BUT
LARGER WINGS CAPABLE OF MAKING FLIGHT COST
ABOUT SIX THOUSAND WITHOUT MOTOR AND
INSTRUMENTS DELIVERY ABOUT THREE MONTHS

Lindbergh wired back, asking if they could cut the construction time to two months.

A Race with Time

Ryan Airlines wired that they could build the plane in two months. On February 23, 1927, Lindbergh arrived by train in San Diego and took a taxi out to the aircraft plant. The first person he met there was a slender young man with a serious look who introduced himself as Donald Hall, chief engineer.

At his drawing board, Hall began to sketch the type of plane he would design to meet the flier's requirements.

"Now, where are we going to put the cockpits for you and the navigator?" Hall asked.

"I only want one cockpit," Lindbergh told him.

The engineer stared at him. "You don't plan on making that flight alone, do you?"

"I'd rather have extra gasoline than an extra man."

Hall became excited. If just one man were aboard the plane, the fuselage could be shorter and therefore lighter. That meant that the ship could carry another 350 pounds of gasoline—about 50 gallons more, including the weight of the tank.

The engineer began to design an aircraft around Lindbergh, all six-foot-three and 170 pounds of him. Crews worked day and night, seven days a week. Sometimes the men put in a 24-hour day. One time Hall worked at his drafting board for 36 hours straight.

Hall had cleared off a table in his drafting room. There, under an unshaded light bulb that hung from the stained ceiling, Lindbergh spread out his charts. The distance from Roosevelt Field to Le Bourget was exactly 3,610 miles. He laid out his course, marking off 100-mile intervals, since the *Spirit of St. Louis* was designed to cruise at about 100 miles an hour. He would adjust his course each hour to allow for wind, storm detours, and the like. Inking in his route, he measured off the time zones.

At last he stood, gazing down at the chart and the graceful curve of the line that ran through New England, Nova Scotia, and

Newfoundland, over the Atlantic, down across the southwestern tip of Ireland, the southwestern tip of England, then to France and Paris—and Le Bourget.

Two incidents in San Diego give a deep insight into the character of Charles A. Lindbergh, his drive for perfection, his determination, and his patience. One was recounted by the flier himself, perhaps without realizing how much it revealed of him. The other came from a Ryan Airlines installation mechanic named O. L. Gray.

The crews had worked for three weeks on the Whirlwind engine and installing it in the nose, Gray said. Then a wrench fell from a mechanic's hip pocket and hit a cylinder, breaking off a cooling fin about the size of a quarter. Lindbergh, Gray recalled, almost cried over that.

"We could smooth that out with a file and paint it, and never know the difference," a mechanic told him.

"I'll always know the difference," Lindbergh pointed out. "We want another engine."

Someone who didn't know what the young flier planned to do with the plane asked, "Why so much perfection in this?"

Lindbergh promptly replied, "Two reasons for that. One is that I'm a poor swimmer. The other reason is that I've always been taught that perfection in your preparation and planning will assure you of getting to your destination."

They took the engine out and installed a new one.*

The other incident, which Lindbergh first described in his account of the flight, *We*, and later in the far more detailed book, *The Spirit of St. Louis*, took place after the construction was completed and he was running his plane through a series of test flights. He was at 1,200 feet, the pilot said, flying over mesquite, when a gust of wind blew his data board out the window.

"All the figures I've collected this morning go fluttering down toward a brush-covered hill below!"

---

* *The American Heritage History of Flight.* (New York: The American Heritage Publishing Company, Inc., 1962).

Lindbergh flying the Spirit of St. Louis.

A Fokker F-10 Super Tri-motor.

He spiraled down, watching the board flashing in the sun. It landed in the top of a mesquite bush, a spot of white among the brownish-green leaves. There was a clearing about two hundred yards from the bush. It was too small to accommodate the *Spirit of St. Louis* but would take a smaller plane.

Flying back to Camp Kearny, whose parade grounds he was using for his runway, he got a slower plane from Ryan, flew to the clearing, and landed.

Leaving the motor turning over, Lindbergh jumped out and put a rock under each wheel to keep the plane from rolling. Then he crawled into the bushes.

So clearly visible from the air, the board was nowhere to be found in the thick mesquite. Removing his coat, Lindbergh spread it over a bush and again took to the air.

There was his coat—and *there*, fifty yards away, was the board. Landing once more, he began to search for the clipboard in relation to his coat, but he couldn't find it. Finally, he moved the coat to where he thought the board should be and took off still another time.

The board, he saw, was just twenty feet from the coat. Once again Lindbergh landed and, after several minutes' search in the mesquite, found the elusive clipboard.

As he went on running more tests, newspapers and the radio continued to report the progress of the other flights. Commander Byrd was planning to fly a huge tri-motor Fokker monoplane from New York to Paris sometime that spring. Sikorsky announced the construction of a second plane for the flight, said to be piloted by René Fonck. The American Legion was backing Commander Noel Davis and Lieutenant Stanton H. Wooster in their big tri-motor ship, the *American Legion*. The owner of the Wright-Bellanca, a monoplane that Lindbergh had once considered buying, also was planning a transatlantic flight.

In France, Captain Charles Nungesser and Lieutenant François Coli announced that they would make the east-west flight. Trans-

*Charles Nungesser
and François Coli
and l'Oiseau Blanc.*

atlantic planes were reportedly under construction in England, France, and Italy.

On April 26, during her final test flight before trying to make Paris, the *American Legion* crashed, and both Davis and Wooster were killed. Also in April, Commander Byrd's Fokker—with the designer himself, Anthony J. Fokker, at the controls—overturned in a landing and three out of four aboard were injured, including Byrd, whose wrist was broken. Floyd Bennett's leg was crushed.

Lindbergh was appalled. All three of the big ships built for the transatlantic flight had crashed. Much as he wanted to be the first to fly to Paris, he didn't wish his rivals bad luck. And those crashes were bad publicity for aviation.

By May 4, Lindbergh was ready to fly the *Spirit of St. Louis* to the city for which she had been named, but day after day he was socked in by fog. Across the continent, across the ocean, Nungesser and Coli took off from Le Bourget Field at sunrise on May 8 in their big biplane, *l'Oiseau Blanc*, the White Bird. It was the first time that an aircraft attempting the actual flight had managed to get off the ground.

At 3:55 P.M. on May 10, with a small suitcase lashed to his fuselage, Lindbergh departed for St. Louis. He arrived at 6:20 A.M. the next day, stayed overnight, and then left for New York at 8:13 A.M. on May 12.

Late that afternoon he passed over the skyscrapers of Manhattan, their myriad windows agleam in the red light of the lowering sun. At 5:33 P.M. he landed at Curtiss Field on Long Island. His elapsed flying time from coast to coast was twenty-one hours and forty-five minutes—a new record.

The Lone Eagle

L'Oiseau Blanc, carrying Nungesser and Coli, was seen crossing southern England. She was seen passing over the southwest coast of Ireland headed out over the Atlantic . . . and she was never seen again.

Lindbergh's response was, "If Nungesser and Coli are lost, it seems to me it's up to the rest of us to carry on what they attempted."

After he landed at Curtiss Field, Lindbergh met Harry Bruno and Richard Blythe, two fliers who handled press relations for Wright Aeronautical Corporation. Earlier that month they had offered their services to Lindbergh gratis, and he had accepted.

Bruno and Blythe were to protect the young pilot against the mob and the exploiters. Their job was difficult in the extreme.

"The obscurity which had until now surrounded the youngster was, even as he landed, forever broken," said Bruno.* That record-breaking coast-to-coast flight had done it. Lindbergh was still the dark horse in the race across the Atlantic, but a dark horse familiar to everyone. The papers carried daily photos and accounts of his activities as he prepared for takeoff. They were already calling him "Lindy" and the "Lone Eagle."

A shy, retiring man, Lindbergh hated the attention. He had no taste for fame. Why was he risking his life in trying to fly the Atlantic? Lindbergh himself has said it was to advance aviation. Harry Bruno, in a personal interview, gave this writer another reason.

"Lindbergh was a very sensitive, thin-skinned kid," Bruno told

---

* Harry Bruno, *Wings Over America* (New York, Robert M. McBride & Company, 1942).

Lindbergh and Harry Bruno.

[18]

me. "As a mail pilot he had been forced to bail out twice from his planes, and he had been ribbed unmercifully by the other pilots. He couldn't take the ribbing. He wanted to prove that he was a better pilot than any of them, that he was the best there was."

His arrival on Long Island spurred the Byrd and Bellanca camps to tremendous efforts to ready their planes for the transatlantic flight. The experts picked Commander Byrd, who was planning a scientific flight with an elite crew, to be the first to succeed.

Next to the favorite was Clarence Chamberlin, a highly skilled pilot who was expected to fly the Wright-Bellanca ship recently christened the *Columbia*.

Flying in, Lindbergh had seen that Curtiss was too small a field to take off from with a full load. Adjacent to Curtiss was Roosevelt Field, with a runway nearly a mile long. Byrd had leased this field and spent a good deal of money improving the runway. Yet he generously let Lindbergh and the *Spirit of St. Louis* use the field when his own plane, the *America*, wasn't.

Stimulated by newspapers, radio, and movie newsreels, public excitement over the flights intensified each day. Already four courageous men had died in the attempt to fly nonstop to Paris; two others were missing and presumed dead. Because he was so young, because he was flying alone in such a small plane, because he was the dark horse, Lindbergh was the center of attention.

Although anxious to get down to business, the Lone Eagle posed for picture after picture and answered endless questions until they got plain silly: "Do you carry a rabbit's foot?" "What's your favorite pie?" "Do you like girls?"

On the evening of May 13 Lindbergh received a telegram:

ARRIVE NEW YORK TOMORROW MORNING

MOTHER

The flier knew what had happened. His mother had been reading and hearing the highly sensational and wildly inaccurate stories in the papers and on the radio. Probably she was being driven to distraction by reporters in Detroit, Michigan, where she

*Lindbergh, Richard E. Byrd,
and Clarence Chamberlin in front
of the* Spirit of St. Louis.

was a high school chemistry teacher, and where he had been born on February 4, 1902.

Lindbergh and his mother were very close. At first strongly opposed to his flying, she had changed so completely that she had barnstormed with him through the Middle West one summer and and often flown his mail route with him, sitting on the mail sacks. With a stoic character like her son, she nonetheless could not help being concerned about what he proposed to do.

Mrs. Lindbergh spent one day with her son, then left for home, assured that he was doing what he wanted to do and that he *knew* what he was doing.

"It was a strange parting," wrote Bruno. "Neither mother nor son showed any emotion."

Even though secure from prying cameras and nosy reporters, they did not embrace. Mrs. Lindbergh patted her son's back and said casually, "Good-bye, Charles. And luck."

"Good-bye, Mother."

"And that," according to Bruno, "was all." *

May 27, when Lindbergh could qualify for the Orteig prize, was still more than a week away. Phoning Harry Knight in St. Louis, Lindbergh pointed this out. The broker did not hesitate:

"To hell with the money. When you're ready to take off, go ahead."

* Bruno, *Wings Over America.*

Mrs. Evangeline Lindbergh and her son.

[23]

A Change of Plan

"Flyin' Fool Adopts Mystery Air, Indicating Quick Take-Off," was the headline in one newspaper on the morning of May 19. Quite the opposite. Weather reports continued to be so bad that Lindbergh left the *Spirit of St. Louis* under guard and drove into New York City. There, Harry Bruno had arranged a dinner for him and some friends at the Newspaper Club on West 42nd Street and had tickets for the hit musical "Rio Rita."

As they drove along 42nd Street about 6:00 P.M., the pavement was shiny with rain and the tops of the skyscrapers were invisible in the mist, but they decided to make a final check with the weather bureau.

The report was good, as good as it would probably be for some time. Swinging the car around, they headed back for Long Island over the Queensboro Bridge. They stopped for a quick supper at a little restaurant near the bridge, and at a drugstore around the corner Dick Blythe bought five sandwiches "to go"—two ham, two roast beef, one hard-boiled egg. These, with a quart canteen of water, were to be Lindbergh's provisions on the flight.

At Curtiss Field, the National Aeronautic Association installed a recording barograph aboard the *Spirit of St. Louis*. The instrument, which marks time and altitude on a revolving paper cylinder, was necessary for the flight to be accepted officially.

Close to midnight Lindbergh went to the nearby Garden City Hotel, where he was staying, to get some sleep. The lobby was filled with reporters, photographers, autograph hounds, promoters, and the usual nuts that gravitate toward celebrities. It was a pandemonium of exploding flashbulbs, screamed questions, curses, demands. With some difficulty Lindbergh managed to escape to his room.

With a friend guarding the door, the young flier undressed and lay down on his bed.

The Spirit of St. Louis
before the flight.

Sleep seemed impossible. He lay awake, thinking about the flight and his last few days in New York. He would be sound asleep now, he knew, if he had been able to work on the *Spirit of St. Louis* during the day.

"That's what I would have been doing except for the newspapers, and the crowds they've brought," he later wrote in a revealing passage. "But I wanted publicity on this flight. That was part of my program. . . . And I knew that headlines bring crowds. Then why should I complain? The excesses are what bother me—the silly stories, the constant photographing . . . the cheap values that such things bring . . ."

The luminous dial on his watch said 1:40. Almost time to go. He lay quietly for a few minutes more, then got up and slowly pulled on his clothes. Night, sleepless night, had passed and dawn was on the way.

Takeoff

"About 7:40 A.M. the motor was started and at 7:52 I took off on the flight for Paris." Thus Lindbergh laconically described his departure in his highly popular account of the flight, *We*. Just like that. Actually, the procedure was considerably more complicated and suspenseful.

"Being young, and easily embarrassed," the Lone Eagle explained much later, "I was hesitant to dwell on my personal errors and sensations. Also, believing in aviation's future, I did not want to lay bare, through my own experience, its existing weaknesses."

When the truck hauled the plane to Roosevelt Field, a light wind was coming out of the east. The truck brought her to the far west end of the runway, and Lindbergh ordered her five fuel tanks topped off. There was a large crowd growing steadily. Somehow the word had got out.

Harry Bruno told me how. "On the evening of May 19 Dick Blythe phoned me at the Newspaper Club to say that Lindbergh was taking off next morning, and suggested that I give the dinner committee some excuse for his absence without revealing the plan," Bruno said. "What we didn't know until later was that a cartoonist from the *Daily Mirror* was in the next booth and overheard our conversation. He of course immediately phoned his city desk. At 9:00 P.M. the *Mirror* was on the street, the newshawks yelling, 'Lindy to take off at dawn!'"

Bruno left Manhattan for Roosevelt Field shortly after midnight in his big yellow convertible. The road to the airfield was filled with about ten thousand cars, moving slowly through the heavy rain.

"As I rode along with them, my hands quivered just the least bit on the wheel," Bruno wrote later. "The same sort of emotions which had gripped me when I made my first flight, when I saw my

Unloading gas for the
Spirit of St. Louis
before the flight.

first plane, returned a thousandfold. I felt . . . that I was steering my car to a rare rendezvous with destiny." *

Bruno's yellow roadster was familiar to the police, and they gave him an escort to where the *Spirit of St. Louis* was being readied. The area around the plane was roped off. "As it grew lighter," Bruno recorded, "we could see that the plane was resting on a glistening bed of violets"**—Napoleon's flower.

Takeoffs and landings are always danger spots in flying, and the police were worried about all that gasoline going into the plane. Bruno arranged to drive behind the *Spirit of St. Louis* as she was going down the runway. In the front seat with him would be Commissioner Abraham Skidmore of the Nassau County Police, holding a fire extinguisher.

Lindbergh shook hands with everyone and climbed into the cockpit. One of the last to tell him goodbye was his generous rival, Commander Byrd . . .

"Off!" Lindbergh shouted to the mechanic. "Throttle closed!"

On the ground the mechanic, Ed Mulligan, pulled the propeller around several times slowly, then yelled, "Contact!"

"Contact!" Lindbergh answered.

Pulling the prop through, Mulligan swung his body away from the blade. The engine caught, sputtering with sharp explosions, then picked up quickly as Lindbergh cracked the throttle. He checked the tachometer on the instrument panel. The prop was spinning at 800 revolutions per minute. The motor was roaring smoothly, all nine cylinders hitting, puffs of blue smoke coming from the exhaust stacks.

Slowly, Lindbergh opened the throttle. The fuselage trembled, and he could feel the wheels push against their blocks. The wings began to quiver. Lindbergh kept opening and closing the throttle. The motor wasn't revving up as it should. It was 30 revolutions

* Bruno, *Wings Over America*.
** Bruno, *Wings Over America*.

[29]

per minute too low, according to the tachometer. The prop was set for cruising, not takeoff.

Lindbergh glanced out at the quivering wings. They would have to lift over 5,000 pounds, a half-ton more than they ever had before, and the prop was spinning 30 r.p.m.'s slow.

Then, to make matters even worse, the fickle wind shifted completely—from east to west, from head to tail, a five-mile-an-hour tail wind. Once a plane is aloft, a tail wind is a great advantage, but it's a serious disadvantage in a takeoff, when a plane needs the resistant buoyancy of the air to become airborne.

Wind, weather, power, load. So many times in the past had he balanced these four elements in his mind. Wind, weather, power, load—and now they were all against him.

If Lindbergh were to take off into the wind, his ship would have to be towed to the other end of the field. (He couldn't taxi there because the light engine pulling the heavy ship over the soft ground would overheat and start to misfire.) The delay could mean that he would hit Ireland after dark, when he couldn't see it. His schedule called for making his landfall there before sunset tomorrow. A westward takeoff would also mean flying at low altitude over hangars and houses—almost sure death if something went wrong.

Mechanics, engineers, policemen, reporters, photographers, and friends all watched Lindbergh tensely. Whether he took off or not was entirely up to him.

"It's less a decision of logic than of feeling," the Lone Eagle explained later, "the kind of feeling that comes when you gauge the distance between two stones across a brook . . ."

He buckled his safety belt, pulled down his goggles, and nodded to the men at the blocks. They yanked them back, freeing the wheels. Lindbergh gave the engine full throttle. The *Spirit of St. Louis*—two and one-half tons with her fuel—started forward

Lindbergh before his takeoff.

[30]

clumsily, "like an overloaded truck." On each side, men were pushing on the wing struts.

"Slowly, too slowly it seemed, the plane started to roll," Bruno wrote. "I swung in behind it in my roadster and off we went. When my speedometer showed just under sixty, the plane, which was lumbering ahead, suddenly left the ground.

"I yelled with relief—only to stifle the yell as the heavily loaded plane hit the ground." *

Down at the end of the runway, getting larger each second, was a steamroller. The *Spirit of St. Louis* sped through a puddle, water shooting up on both sides, drumming on the fuselage. The runway became a blur. Answering her pilot's pressure on the stick, the *Spirit of St. Louis* rose a second time, took a longer hop, then touched lightly, "a last bow to earth" in Lindbergh's phrase, and was airborne.

She cleared the steamroller by fifteen feet. Her pilot kept pulling back on the stick. High-tension wires ahead. She cleared them by twenty feet. High trees on a hill dead ahead. No chance of clearing them. Lindbergh kicked the right rudder pedal and the *Spirit of St. Louis* banked to the right.

"How he missed that steamroller and those wires, I'll never know," Bruno told me. "At the end of the runway I slammed on the brakes. For several minutes Commissioner Skidmore and I just sat there, too worked up to say a word. Then we looked at each other and exclaimed in unison, 'By God, he made it!' "

It was 7:52 A.M. Lindbergh unfolded a map of New York and spread it on his knees. Ahead of the *Spirit of St. Louis* was the serene water of Long Island Sound, then Connecticut—flat and blue in the distance. Two planes with newspaper photographers that had been following Lindbergh dipped their wings and turned back. The Lone Eagle flew alone.

* Bruno, *Wings Over America*.

The Last of America

8:52 A.M. The first hour of flight was over. Lindbergh wrote down in his log:

VISIBILITY: 5 miles
ALTITUDE: 600 feet
AIRSPEED: 102 m.p.h.

The *Spirit of St. Louis* passed over Rhode Island in less than twenty minutes. Her pilot put that map away and unfolded the one of Massachusetts—the fourth state map he had opened since the start of his flight about an hour and a quarter ago. Ahead was the Atlantic.

It looked quite calm—not hostile at all. He brought his plane down to about twenty feet, then to about six feet, above the gentle waves. Close to the ground or a body of water, he knew, is a cushion of air through which a plane passes more easily than at a greater height. But after a while, flying low became tiresome, and he took her up to one hundred feet.

10:52 A.M. Four hours out. The engine, which burned sixteen gallons of fuel an hour, had lightened the ship by about 300 pounds. His wool-lined flying suit was uncomfortably hot. He unzipped it, but kept it on. His legs were stiff and aching. He knew from long experience in flying the mail, however, that after about seven hours the pain would go away.

Sleep was a treacherous enemy that began to grow stronger with each hour. He cupped his hand into the slipstream and deflected the cold air into his face.

A great green landmass appeared on the horizon. Going up to 1,000 feet, Lindbergh unfolded his map of Nova Scotia and compared it with the low grassy shoreline below. He had made his landfall at the mouth of St. Mary's Bay—just six miles off course.

Cloud formations over the Atlantic.

In laying the course out in San Diego, he had figured an error of five degrees would be allowable, but he had kept within *two*.

Lunchtime. "I drop my hand to the bag of sandwiches, but I'm not hungry. Why eat simply because it's lunchtime?"

He took a sip of water for lunch.

In hanging up the canteen, he nearly let his chart flutter out the window like that data board in San Diego. Frantically, he snatched the priceless chart back. He thought of the humiliating explanation he would have to make: "On course, plenty of fuel, all readings normal, but the chart blew out the window."

Slowly the sky began to fill: a few stray cumulus clouds, then great herds of them. A dark mass of clouds on his left obliterated the northern horizon. Thick slanting gray shafts broke up the horizon ahead—rain squalls.

The *Spirit of St. Louis* began to bump and buck. Lakes he passed over were choppy, whipped by a gale. The wings began to jerk.

The first squall was not very big, but each one that followed was worse, filled with heavy rain, streaks of lightning, and the splintering crash of thunder. Lindbergh decided to give up his course for the time being and turned east, hoping to slip past the edges of the worst storms.

Whenever possible, he returned to his course, leaving it when the violence around him grew too great. Gradually the wind swung around from northwest to southeast, from head wind to tail wind. A good sign.

Then fog, an enemy almost as dangerous to a flier as sleep, appeared ahead. Like a great white rug it covered the land below him, rendering all checkpoints invisible. Because he was navigating by dead reckoning, he had to know his exact position before he dared venture any further. If he couldn't learn his exact position, he had no choice but to turn back.

Then ahead he saw the blue Atlantic sparkling in the sunlight; and below, through the shredding fog, was Chedabucto Bay and Cape Breton Island.

[35]

Lindbergh debated with himself whether to deviate a bit to the south so as to pass over St. John's, the capital of Newfoundland. He would like the word to get back to his mother and partners and everyone else that he had passed St. John's.

On the other hand, he had drawn quite a bit on his fuel reserves by detouring around the squalls over Nova Scotia. He would need every gallon of gas he had aboard.

But what if he had to make a forced landing in the Atlantic? It would greatly enhance his chances of being rescued if the searchers knew he had gone down somewhere east of St. John's.

"If I can't charge a gallon of fuel to sentiment," he thought, "I *can* charge it to safety."

Lindbergh kicked right rudder and his ship banked, heading south. Behind him the sun was setting. The *Spirit of St. Louis* flew into the gathering night.

Sleep came into the cockpit. Lindbergh's eyes closed. With a great effort, he forced them open. The cramps in his legs had left, as he had known they would. To keep his mind sharp, he concentrated on difficulties lying ahead. What if the wind shifted and blew him off course? Or, what if Europe was covered with fog?

The Atlantic ahead was bright and gleaming white—an ice field, a fleet of icebergs creeping south. The eerie sight, the eerie light, revived him. Any change, he realized, stimulates the senses. To fight sleep, he must fly high for a while, then low, use his left hand on the stick, then his right, sipping water from time to time.

Having burned nine hours of fuel, the *Spirit of St. Louis* was 800 pounds lighter and responded to the slightest pressure on the stick. Lindbergh was having trouble keeping the compass needle centered. Sleep was back. Below, the ice field slipped away, and the Atlantic ahead was a wilderness of heaving waves. The air was cold and biting.

At 5:52 P.M. the *Spirit of St. Louis* was over Placentia Bay, Newfoundland. Lindbergh took her down low over the granite mountains.

[36]

"What joy it is to fly past crags like an eagle, to glide fearlessly over the edge of these great cliffs. From now on, the explosion of the engine will be inseparable from the beat of my heart. As I trust one, I'll trust the other."

Day was ending, and the last of America was slipping past. The *Spirit of St. Louis* swooped down over St. John's, then headed toward night and Ireland, 2,000 miles away. She was the first aircraft making an eastward flight to pass over St. John's without landing.

Into the Thunderhead

Fog. It came at him in tatters and patches at first, then turned into a white wall. Conditions were zero zero, no ceiling and no visibility. Blind flying, the deadly monotony of lining up one needle after another on the instrument board, was an invitation for sleep to come back into the cockpit, and stay.

He pulled back on the stick and the *Spirit of St. Louis* climbed until the altimeter needle pointed to 10,000 feet, but the ship was just skimming the white floor. He was flying past mountains of clouds, huge pillars of mist that rose thousands of feet above the mass—and above him—higher than any cloud formations he had ever known.

All at once he was aware of pain in the top of his head. His head, for some reason, was pressing against the cabin roof. It took him a few seconds to figure out why . . . Of course. The air cushion he was sitting on was expanding as his plane climbed to diminishing atmospheric pressure. He let out some air, and the pain went away.

Dead ahead a great cloud column blacked out the stars, flattening on top like a giant mushroom—a thunderhead. Lindbergh tightened his seat belt, pushed the nose down a bit, and flew into the thunderhead.

The wings began to quiver. The *Spirit of St. Louis* was jolted and jerked about. Everything was black except for the luminescent dials on his instrument panel and the red flare of the engine's exhaust on the rushing fog. It was bitter cold in the cabin. Lindbergh pulled off a leather mitten and stuck his arm out the window. Tiny jabs stung his hand.

Sleet. He pulled out his flashlight and threw a beam onto a wing strut. The beam, like a long yellow tube, was shot through with thousands of shiny white streaks. It showed ice on the strut.

The ship was icing up and soon would be dangerously heavy and hard to maneuver.

He had to get out of here, and fast—but not too fast. Although his entire body was screaming for a steep bank and dive out of the thunderhead, Lindbergh's iron mind maintained command.

"It's easy enough to get into a steep bank, but more difficult to get out of one," he told himself. ". . . The plane may get entirely out of control."

Carefully he dipped a wing and brought his ship around until she flew out of the deadly thunderhead the same way she had come in.

Then he began to follow valleys and canyons in the mist mountains. But flying around the sleety walls of the thunderheads, he was burning fuel he could not afford. He had picked up no telling how much ice. It was making the *Spirit of St. Louis* sluggish.

The passes were beginning to narrow. Looking ahead, Lindbergh saw more towering black masses. What if they came together in one great icy fortress? For the first time since he had taken off from Roosevelt Field 15 hours ago, he thought of turning back. In spite of his determination he was close to being incapable of keeping his fragile craft from spinning down into the waves. Fog, ice, sleep, and fatigue were joining forces to overwhelm him. He was losing control. In the fuselage behind his back, phantoms were talking to him with great authority, but he could not remember a word they said.

"If my plane can stay aloft," he told himself, "if my engine can keep on running, then so can I."

His fuel, however, was as vital to him as his own blood, and every hour the engine was burning up sixteen gallons. When that fuel was gone, the engine would sputter and die. Then skill, courage, and iron will added up to zero-zero-zero in keeping the *Spirit of St. Louis* aloft.

Suddenly both compasses began to swing wildly, making no sense whatsoever. Dull as his mind had become, Lindbergh soon grasped the reason. On top of everything else, he was flying through a magnetic storm. But he must have the use of his compasses. Without their honest testimony, how could he tell—how in the world could he tell—whether he was heading for Ireland—or Greenland?

A Whiff of Ammonia

On the left a whitish glimmer in the clouds. He had almost forgotten his friend, the moon. Now, as it rose higher in the northeast and its light grew stronger, it showed him the fantastic cloud country he was flying across. It was as though he were in a sacred garden, a forbidden temple. On both sides of him towered high cloud walls as he followed the lighted passageway ahead.

The moon was so bright he could almost read his chart by it. The air was warmer. He could see that the ice was gone completely from his struts. He must be over the Gulf Stream. A man could live quite a long time in a raft in the Gulf Stream, he told himself.

For such an emergency he was carrying aboard the *Spirit of St. Louis* five tins of army rations and a canteen containing a gallon of water.

In the east he saw a pink glow. Dawn? The clock on his instrument panel said 1:00 A.M. But that was New York time. The glow was dawn all right.

Now sleep assaulted him as never before, as if earlier attacks had all been feints. On the instrument panel the compass needle began to wander. He kicked left rudder, then right rudder, forcing that gypsy needle back into line. He had to watch the *Spirit of St. Louis* like a hawk. Otherwise she would start to misbehave "like a spoiled child piqued at a moment's neglect." He was glad, however, that she was not a stable ship. Her constant veering off course and the necessity of guiding her back kept him awake, and alive.

Lindbergh used every trick he had ever learned to fight sleep. He tensed his muscles, shook himself, bounced up and down in his seat, pried his eyelids open with his fingers. He dipped one wing, then the other, to bring blasts of fresh air into the cabin. He knew that if he could stay aloft and on course for one more hour, the sun would be over the eastern horizon and he would be all right.

1:52 A.M. The nineteenth hour.

Behind him were 1,800 miles. Ahead were 1,800 miles. He had planned a celebration when he came to this point, like having a sandwich. But although he had eaten nothing since takeoff, he still wasn't hungry, and he wasn't thirsty either. He switched on the nose tank and turned off the fuselage tank.

He had reached the point of no return. Before, safety had lain behind him, in the west. Now it lay before him, in Europe.

Fog ahead. The *Spirit of St. Louis* burrowed into it. Lindbergh put her nose down, leveling out at 8000 feet, searching the cloud floor below him for an opening. Then "like a rare stone perceived among countless pebbles," he saw the blue-gray ocean. Lindbergh pushed the vibrating stick forward and his plane nosed down. With the change in pressure, his ears popped, cleared, popped again, and his air cushion shriveled until he could feel the ribs of the cut-down wicker chair that was his flying seat.

He kept descending until the cockpit was filled with spray, until the waves were breaking just a few feet below his wheels. The waves were huge, their tops foaming whitecaps. From the direction of the blown spray, he saw that the wind was from the northwest, still a tail wind. But where was he?

He pushed the stick forward and to one side to lift the wing and bathed his face in the slipstream. It came to him then that he had at last defeated his enemy. He was completely awake, entirely alert.

"How beautiful the ocean is; how clear the sky; how fiery the sun! Whatever coming hours hold, it's enough to be alive this minute."

He was still utterly in the dark, however, about his position. During the night he could have strayed hundreds of miles off course. If so, shouldn't he throttle down to save fuel? "But if security were my prime motive, I'd never have begun this flight at all—I'd never have learned to fly in the first place."

He speeded up the engine, giving it a richer mixture of gasoline, and saw the airspeed indicator rise from 93 to 100 m.p.h.

He was beginning to get drowsy again. In his medical kit he

found a capsule of aromatic ammonia. One whiff should revive him. He broke the capsule in his fingers and held it gingerly to his nose and inhaled. He felt nothing. He held it directly under his nostrils and took a deep breath. Again, nothing.

He tossed the capsule out the window. He was beginning to realize just how low his reserves were, how dull his senses.

"Which Way Is Ireland?"

During the twenty-seventh hour of flight, Lindbergh sighted a dark speck several miles to the southeast. As he drew closer, the speck separated into several specks and then became small fishing boats. They meant Europe was near. He flew low over the first boat without seeing any sign of life. As he circled the second boat, however, a man's face appeared in a cabin porthole.

Lindbergh had been able to hold brief conversations with people on the ground while flying by throttling back on his motor. He swooped down within a few feet of the boat, throttled the engine, and shouted, "Which way is Ireland?"

No answer. The fisherman just gawked at him. The *Spirit of St. Louis* lost airspeed and was in danger of crashing into the waves. Lindbergh gunned the motor, and his ship zoomed up.

Nearly an hour later he saw what looked like land, a purplish-blue stretch between two gray columns of rain on his left, and he banked in that direction. If it *was* land, if it was Ireland, he was two and a half hours ahead of schedule. As he drew closer, he saw a vivid green semimountainous coastline coming down from the north, curving over toward the west. It had a series of long narrow inlets like the fjords of Norway. Unfolding his map of Ireland, Lindbergh compared it with the land below. He found Cape Valentia and Dingle Bay. He was flying over the southwestern tip of Ireland.

It was incredible. Laying out his course in San Diego, he had figured he would be doing well if he hit Ireland within fifty miles of his course. He had made his landfall within *three* miles. He swooped low over a little village. People ran out into the roads, waving at him.

Over St. George's Channel, he decided to let the nose tank run until dry to give his ship a heavier tail. If he was forced down, there would be less chance of her nosing over. The worst was behind him. From now on, it was all downhill.

The *Spirit of St. Louis* began to jerk; the engine that had performed perfectly since takeoff was sputtering. Lindbergh prepared to ditch in the Channel, looking about for a ship to land near.

But of course. The nose tank had run dry, as he had intended it to. He switched that tank off and turned on the center wing tank. The engine smoothed out and its power swept through the *Spirit of St. Louis.*

Soon Land's End, the southwestern tip of England, appeared on one horizon, then disappeared on the other, and the plane was flying over the choppy English Channel. On his right the sun was setting.

Up ahead, he saw land: Cape de la Hague. France!

He was about three hours ahead of schedule, having averaged better than 100 miles an hour during the whole flight. The clock on the instrument panel said 4:20, which meant 9:20 French time—way past suppertime. Lindbergh opened the bag and took out a meat sandwich, his first food since takeoff yesterday morning. It didn't taste very good, but he was hungry. He started to throw the wrapping out the window, then put it back in the bag. He didn't want to mar such an auspicious occasion by littering.

He felt great, wide awake, completely free of aches and fatigue. He wanted to sit quietly in his cockpit and let the full realization of his feat sink in.

Flying at 4,000 feet, he saw a glow ahead. Paris, the City of Light, was rising over the horizon like the moon. Near the center, marked by a column of lights was the Eiffel Tower. He circled it, then turned northeast toward Le Bourget.

The field was all lit up. Lindbergh spiraled down, flew low over it once, then circled into the wind and landed. It was 10:24 P.M. Paris time, thirty-three and one-half hours after takeoff. Turning the *Spirit of St. Louis* around, Lindbergh started to taxi for the hangars, but the entire field ahead was an incoming tide of men,

Lindbergh being driven from Le Bourget.

women, and children—perhaps 100,000 strong, perhaps more—sprinting toward him, shouting at the top of their lungs.

"*Vive* Lindbergh! Long live Lindbergh!"

Before the whirling prop killed someone, the Lone Eagle cut the switch. Seconds later the mob closed in. The *Spirit of St. Louis* began to crack in places from the pressure. Before she got broken up, Lindbergh started to climb out of the cockpit to draw the people off. He got one foot out the door; then he was dragged the rest of the way.

"For nearly half an hour I was unable to touch the ground," Lindbergh wrote later; the screaming Frenchmen carried him around the field on their shoulders. Then two French military pilots came to his rescue. Snatching off his leather helmet, they stuck it on the head of an American newspaper correspondent and shouted, "Here's Lindbergh!"

The helmet did the trick. The crowd grabbed the protesting correspondent and marched him off to the reception committee. Meanwhile the two pilots took the Lone Eagle to the American Embassy.

At 4:15 A.M. on May 22, the reporters had finished asking their questions and Lindbergh could go to bed. It had been sixty-three hours since he had last slept.

When he awoke the next afternoon, he wanted to fly to London and use the new transatlantic telephone to call his mother. A special wire, he learned, had been run from England to Paris just so he could make the call. What was said in this unique conversation is known only to him—and to her.

Afterwards

Some of the frenzied enthusiasm with which the French greeted Lindbergh might be explained by the name of his plane. Although St. Louis is not the patron saint of France (that honor belongs to St. Denis), nor of Paris (that is St. Genevieve), St. Louis—King Louis IX—who ruled France during much of the thirteenth century and in whose reign she enjoyed unprecedented peace and prosperity, is revered by all Frenchmen. It is doubtful that they would have been as worked up over the arrival of a plane named the *America* or the *Columbia*.

However, the display of strong feeling shown at Le Bourget Field was repeated in Belgium, where Lindbergh next visited, then England, and finally the United States. Everywhere he went he received honors and the accolades of the public. As Frederick Lewis Allen observes in *Only Yesterday*, "Something that people needed, if they were to live at peace with themselves and the rest of the world, was missing from their lives. And all at once Lindbergh provided it. Romance, chivalry, self-dedication—here they were embodied in a modern Galahad for a generation which had foresworn Galahads."

There were many inaccuracies printed about his flight. "Well, I made it," were his first words upon landing, according to one paper. Another said they were, "Well, here we are." A third, "Am I here?"

Lindbergh himself states flatly that he said none of these things. His first words, which probably nobody heard in the brouhaha anyhow, were, "Are there any mechanics here?" His next words, "Does anyone here speak English?" got a response no more intelligible to him than the first. But everything Lindbergh did and said was news, even if he didn't do or say it.

However, his speech to a group of deputies of the French

Lindbergh after his flight across the Atlantic.

Chamber was reported correctly and revealed his view of his own accomplishment.

". . . skeptics might ask me what good has been my flight from New York to Paris. My answer is that I believe it is the forerunner of a great air service from America to France, America to Europe, to bring our peoples nearer together in understanding and in friendship than they have ever been."

His modesty and sincerity made a deep impression upon his listeners.

President Coolidge sent the cruiser U.S.S. *Memphis* to Cherbourg, France, to bring the Lone Eagle home to his mother, more medals—including the Congressional Medal of Honor—and the adoration of millions. In the parade up Broadway in New York City alone, an estimated 1,800 tons of ticker tape, torn-up phone books, and other paper was showered on the returning hero, as a skywriter wrote, "HAIL LINDY."

Raymond Orteig decided to waive the sixty-day waiting period, and on June 16, 1927, he presented the Lone Eagle with the $25,000 prize. The following week Lindbergh went to Dayton, Ohio, for a quiet visit with Orville Wright (Wilbur Wright had died in 1912 of typhoid fever).

The *Spirit of St. Louis* had come home with Lindbergh aboard U.S.S. *Memphis*. In August, while flying her around the nation to promote commercial aviation, he took Henry Ford up for a hop, the Detroit automobile manufacturer's first plane ride.

An avalanche of congratulatory telegrams, cables, and letters descended upon the flier. The United States and the world took

Lindbergh on board
the U.S.S. Memphis,
returning to
the United States.

Lindbergh to their hearts as probably no other hero in history. He had performed a feat many men had attempted before him with no success. He had flown nonstop from New York to Paris, and he had done it *alone*.

Significance of the Flight

When Orville Wright flew at Kitty Hawk in 1903, there were only five witnesses, and newspapers had no interest in the feat whatsoever. As late as 1905, the prestigious *Scientific American* magazine mentioned the flight only to suggest that it was a hoax.

In the quarter-century between that flight and Lindbergh's, aeronautics was still mainly a matter of stunting and thrills at carnivals and county fairs, like ballooning in the previous century. The aerial dogfights over the trenches in World War I had given the conflict some glamour. The general public, however, still fascinated by the automobile, did not consider the airplane a means of transportation.

Lindbergh changed all that. The impact of his flight was explosive. It is estimated that newspapers used more than 25,000 tons of newsprint in May and June of 1927 in reporting the flight. Radio stations broadcast news of Lindbergh's activities from coast to coast and around the world.

In 1927, a total of 8,661 people traveled by air in the United States. The very next year the number of air travelers jumped to 47,000. By the end of 1928 there were forty-eight air routes established in the United States. That year American airline operators doubled their 1927 mileage and tripled their mail load, besides nearly quadrupling their passengers. In 1928, applications for pilot's licenses in the U.S. leaped from 1,800 to 5,500.

"The six months which followed the Lindbergh flight were about the craziest six months in the history of aviation," wrote Harry Bruno. "Fliers who had planned their ocean hops before Lindbergh now accelerated their preparations. Aviators who had never dreamed of flying across a body of water bigger than the lake in [New York City's] Central Park now rushed to prospective sponsors with pleas for ocean-spanning planes. And notoriety seek-

[53]

The only newspaper in Washington with the Associated Press news every morning in the year.

The Washi

NO. 18,602.

ENTERED AS SECOND-CLASS MATTER POSTOFFICE, WASHINGTON, D. C.

WASHINGTON: SUNDAY, MAY

LINDBERGH WILDLY H
FOR 3,800-MILE FLI
AIRMAN TELLS

LONE FLIER W

SLEET AND MIST CHIEF HANDICAPS OVER THE OCEAN

Sitting in Bed at American Embassy Flier Tells of Long Hours of Blind Progress Through Night and Day on Epochal Voyage.

ATE SANDWICH AND A HALF ON THE WAY; DRANK SOME WATER AND SLEPT LITTLE

Flew High at Times, He Says, and Barely Cleared Waves at Others While Trying to Avoid Storm; Almost Crushed in Crowd; Fell and Felt Feet on His Back.

By HENRY WALES.
(Special Cable Dispatch.)

Paris, Sunday, May 22.—At 1 o'clock this morning Capt. Charles A. Lindbergh, with M. Weiss, veteran French pilot, escaped from the hangar at Le Bourget and stealthily crossed the air field aboard an automobile and was whirled to Paris by roundabout roads to escape the glut of cars on the main high-

~~jton~~ Post.

Weather—Partly cloudy and slightly warmer today; tomorrow cloudy; moderate southeast and south winds. Temperature yesterday—Highest, 75; lowest, 57.

Weather details on page 18.

27.—NINETY-EIGHT PAGES   ✳   COPYRIGHT, 1927, BY THE WASHINGTON POST CO.   **FIVE CENTS.**

ILED AT PARIS
HT IN 33½ HOURS;
WN STORY OF TRIP

AZED TRAIL ACROSS ATLANTIC

HERO IS MOBBED BY VAST THRONG ON FRENCH FIELD

"Well, Here We Are" He Says Wearily as Plane Is Brought Down Safely at End of the First Nonstop Air Trip From New York.

GREATEST EVENT IN AVIATION HISTORY, EXPERTS ASSERT; ALL PRAISE HIS DARING

Crowd of 25,000 Lifts Him From Machine as It Stops; Feat Wins $25,000 Orteig Prize Offered by Frenchman for First Aviator Across.

Paris, May 21 (By A. P.).—Capt. Charles A. Lindbergh, the young American aviator, who hopped off from New York yesterday morning all alone in his monoplane, arrived in Paris tonight, safe and sound, as everyone hoped he would.

The sandy-haired son of the middle West dropped down out of the darkness at Le Bourget flying field, a few miles from Paris, at 10:21 o'clock tonight (4:21 p. m. eastern standard

ers who had never sat in an airplane before now tried to join projected flights even as dead baggage." *

The first man to fly the Atlantic after Lindbergh was Clarence D. Chamberlin in the *Columbia*, June 4–6, that same year. Aiming at Berlin, Germany, he ran out of fuel 118 miles short of the capital and crash-landed in an oatfield (neither he nor his passenger, the owner of the plane, were injured). Commander Byrd's *America* took off for Rome on June 29, ran out of gas fighting bad weather, and crash-landed in the sea off Brest, France. All aboard made it to shore.

Within a year eighteen planes tried the west-east Atlantic crossing. Seven succeeded. Failures cost the lives of eleven men and one woman. Thirteen flights from Europe to America were attempted during the same period. Only three made it. Five men and three women gave their lives in the unsuccessful attempts. Some planes were forced to turn back because of bad weather.

Those failures reaffirmed the savage nature of the Atlantic and underscored Lindbergh's triumph. He had proved once and for all that the airplane was capable of everything that the pioneers claimed. Transatlantic flights at first were available to carry the mail, and in 1939 passenger service began. The flight of the Lone Eagle had launched the Air Age.

* Bruno, *Wings Over America*.

Bibliography

Allen, Frederick Lewis. *Only Yesterday*. New York: Harper & Brothers, 1931.
———. *The Big Change*. New York: Harper & Brothers, 1952.
The American Heritage History of Flight. New York: The American Heritage Publishing Company, Inc., 1962.
Asimov, Isaac. *Asimov's Biographical Encyclopedia of Science and Technology*. Garden City: Doubleday & Company, Inc., 1964.
Bruno, Harry. *Wings Over America*. New York: Robert M. McBride & Company, 1942.
Calitri, Princine. *Harry A. Bruno, Public Relations Pioneer*. Minneapolis: T. S. Denison & Company, Inc., 1968.
Dictionary of American Biography. New York: Charles Scribner's Sons, 1935.
Encyclopaedia Britannica. Chicago: The University of Chicago Press, 1944.
Family Almanac. New York: The New York Times, 1972.
Graff, Henry F. *The Free and The Brave, The Story of The American People*. Chicago: Rand McNally & Company, 1967.
Lindbergh, Charles A. *The Spirit of St. Louis*. New York: Charles Scribner's Sons, 1953.
———. *We*. New York: G. P. Putnam's Sons, 1927.
Mason, Herbert Molloy, Jr. *Bold Men, Far Horizons*. Philadelphia: J. B. Lippincott Company, 1966.
Ross, Walter S. *The Last Hero: Charles A. Lindbergh*. New York: Harper & Row, 1964.

Index

About the Author

John T. Foster is the author of a number of books for young readers. A graduate of Florida Southern College, he also studied at the University of Florida and the University of Wisconsin. He spent many years in newspaper work in Florida, Louisiana, and New York. He is now technical editor at the New York Ocean Science Laboratory in Montauk, New York. His other books include The Gallant Gray Trotter, Napoleon's Marshal, and The Hundred Days.